Fulham

Quiz Book

101 Fun and Interesting Questions
To Test Your Knowledge
Of Fulham Football Club

Published by Glowworm Press
7 Nuffield Way
Abingdon OX14 1RL

By Chris Carpenter

Fulham Football Club

This Fulham Football Club quiz book contains one hundred and one informative and entertaining trivia questions with multiple choice answers. Some of the questions are easy, and some are challenging, and this book is guaranteed to test your knowledge of **Fulham Football Club**.

You will be asked a large variety of questions on a wide range of topics associated with Fulham FC for you to test yourself. You will be quizzed on players, managers, opponents, transfer deals, records, fixtures and more, guaranteeing you an educational experience and plenty of fun. Both informative and enjoyable, this quiz book will give you the chance to prove you know your club's history and is a must-have for all loyal Fulham supporters.

2020/21 Season Edition

FOREWORD

When I was asked to write a foreword to this book I was deeply honoured.

I have known the author Chris Carpenter for many years and his knowledge of facts and figures is phenomenal.

His love for South West London and his huge talent for writing quiz books make him the ideal man to pay homage to my great love Fulham Football Club.

This book came about as a result of a challenge in a Lebanese restaurant of all places!

I do hope you enjoy the book.

Simon Haynes

Let's start with some relatively easy questions.

1. When was Fulham founded?
   A. 1877
   B. 1878
   C. 1879

2. Where do Fulham play their home games?
   A. Craven Cottage
   B. Swiss Cottage
   C. White Cottage

3. What is Fulham's nickname?
   A. The Artisans
   B. The Cottagers
   C. The Rivermen

4. What will the stadium's capacity be once the Riverside Stand is completed?
   A. 25,600
   B. 27,600
   C. 29,600

5. Who or what is the club mascot?
   A. Billy The Badger
   B. Billy The Bat
   C. Billy The Beefeater

6. Who has made the most appearances for the club in total?
   A. Les Barratt
   B. Johnny Haynes
   C. Eddie Lowe

7. Who is the club's record goal scorer?
   A. Gordon Davies
   B. Johnny Haynes
   C. Rodney Marsh

8. What is the official Fulham website address?
   A. fulham.com
   B. fulhamfc.com
   C. fulhamweb.com

9. Which of the following songs do the players run out to?
   A. Amadeus
   B. Nessun Dorma
   C. Palladio

10. Which of these is a well known pub near the ground?
    A. The Golden Lion
    B. The Red Lion
    C. The White Lion

Here are the answers to the first ten questions. If you get seven or more right, you are doing well, but the questions will get harder.

A1. Fulham were formed on the 18th August 1879 as Fulham St Andrews Church Sunday School FC.

A2. Fulham play their home games at the very atmospheric Craven Cottage.

A3. Fulham's nickname is officially the Cottagers, although they are also known as the Whites or Lilywhites.

A4. Prior to redevelopment of The Riverside Stand, the capacity was 25,700 and once the development is finished the capacity will increase to 29,600 – all seated. It is going to be great.

A5. The club mascot is of course Billy the Badger. If you're a golfer, you may be interested to know you can buy a Billy the Badger head cover from the club shop, and also from Amazon.

A6. Johnny Haynes made the most appearances for the club. He played in 658 first-team matches in total in his 19 year career at the club.

A7. Gordon Davies is Fulham's record goal scorer with 159 goals in all competitions.

A8. The official Fulham website can be found at fulhamfc.com and a very useful site it is too.

A9. The players run out to Palladio, the first track on a 1996 album by Welsh composer Karl Jenkins. Specifically it is Palladio I, Allegretto. The piece has also been used by De Beers diamonds in various different arrangements to support their TV adverts. It has also been sampled by others including Escala, which is why it may sound so familiar.

A10. The Golden Lion is a well known pub near Putney Bridge tube station. Be prepared to queue for a pint though.

OK, back to the questions.

11. Who won the 2010 League Manager of the Year Award?
    A. Paul Bracewell
    B. Roy Hodgson
    C. Martin Jol

12. What position did Fulham finish in their first ever Premier League campaign?
    A. 13th
    B. 15th
    C. 17th

13. Which Fulham player played in a World Cup Final?
    A. Alan Ball
    B. George Cohen
    C. Ray Wilson

14. Who has made the most league appearances for the club?
    A. George Cohen
    B. Johnny Haynes
    C. Frank Penn

15. What is the traditional home end of the ground?
    A. Hammersmith End
    B. Putney End
    C. World's End

16. What is the club's record attendance?

A. 47,115
B. 48,225
C. 49,335

17. Where is Fulham's training ground?
    A. Finch Park
    B. Motspur Park
    C. Thrush Park

18. What is the name of the road that Craven Cottage is on?
    A. Orphanage Road
    B. Stevenage Road
    C. Vicarage Road

19. Which stand has the biggest capacity?
    A. Hammersmith End
    B. Johnny Haynes Stand
    C. Putney End

20. What is the size of the pitch?
    A. 105x75 yards
    B. 110x70 yards
    C. 110x75 yards

Here are the answers to the last set of questions.

A11. The League Manager of The Year award is voted for by fellow managers and the winner can come from any of the four professional leagues. Roy Hodgson was the well deserved winner in 2010 - winning by a record margin.

A12. Fulham finished a very respectable 13th in the club's first ever season in the Premier League in 2001/02.

A13. Described by George Best as "the best full back I have ever played against" George Cohen was a member of the England 1966 World Cup winning side. He made 459 appearances for Fulham and won 39 England caps.

A14. Johnny Haynes made 594 league appearances for the club in total. Legend

A15. Three stands are reserved for home supporters only, but the Hammersmith End is the traditional "home end" of the ground.

A16. Fulham's record home attendance is 49,335 against Millwall on 8th October 1933.

A17. Fulham's training ground is located at Motspur Park in New Malden.

A18. Craven Cottage is on Orphanage Road.

A19. The Hammersmith End currently has the largest capacity, being able to accommodate 7,769 people, and the second largest is the Putney End which can seat 7,281 people. When the Riverside Stand is complete, that will become the biggest stand being able to accommodate 8,650 people.

A20. The size of the pitch is 110 yards long by 75 yards wide. By way of comparison, Wembley's pitch is 115 yards long by 75 yards wide

Let's move onto the next set of questions.

21. What is the club's record win in any
    competition?
    A. 8-1
    B. 9-1
    C. 10-1

22. Who did they beat?
    A. Ipswich Town
    B. Norwich City
    C. Peterborough United

23. In which season?
    A. 1961/62
    B. 1962/63
    C. 1963/64

24. What is the club's record win in the Premier
    League?
    A. 5-0
    B. 6-1
    C. 6-0

25. Who was the designer/architect of Craven
    Cottage?
    A. James Gillespie
    B. Archibald Leitch
    C. Robert McAlpine

26. Who is currently the Chief Executive Officer of
    the club?
    A. Karim Fayed

B. Alistair Mackintosh
C. Mark Lampling

27. What is the club's record defeat?
    A. 0-8
    B. 0-9
    C. 0-10

28. Who against?
    A. Liverpool
    B. Manchester United
    C. Manchester City

29. How many points did Fulham win in running away with the Football League Division One title in 2000/01?
    A. 97
    B. 99
    C. 101

30. Who was the manager of the record breaking 2000/01 side?
    A. Micky Adams
    B. Kevin Keegan
    C. Jean Tigana

Here are the answers to the last set of questions.

A21. The club's record win in any competition is 10-1.

A22. The record 10-1 win came against Ipswich Town - in the First Division.

A23. The match took place on Boxing Day - 26th December 1963, so it was the 1963/64 season.

A24. The club's record win in the Premier League is 6-0. They thrashed Norwich City on 15th May 2005 and also beat QPR by the same score on the 2nd November 2011.

A25. Craven Cottage was designed by Archibald "Archie" Leitch, Britain's foremost football architect.

A26. Alistair Mackintosh is the current CEO. He joined the club in the summer of 2008 from Manchester City.

A27. The club's record defeat in any competition is 0-10.

A28. Liverpool beat Fulham 10-0 in a League Cup match on the 23rd September 1986.

A29. At the end of the 2000/01 season, Fulham were crowned champions with 101 points, at the time a record, with a 10 point margin over runners-up Blackburn Rovers.

A30. Jean Tigana was the manager that fabulous season back in 2000/01.

Here is the next set of questions.

31. What is the club's best ever finish in the
    league?
    A. 7th
    B. 8th
    C. 9th

32. Who was the manager as Fulham recorded
    their best ever league finish?
    A. Chris Coleman
    B. Roy Hodgson
    C. Kevin Keegan

33. How many points did Fulham finish with at the
    end of their record setting 2008/09 season?
    A. 51
    B. 52
    C. 53

34. When did the club win the Intertoto Cup?
    A. 1998
    B. 2000
    C. 2002

35. Who did they beat in the final?
    A. Bologna
    B. Napoli
    C. Torino

36. What was the score?
    A. 2-0
    B. 3-1

C. 5-3

37. How many times have Fulham reached the
semi finals of the FA Cup?
    A. 4
    B. 5
    C. 6

38. How many times have Fulham reached the FA
Cup final?
    A. 0
    B. 1
    C. 2

39. In the run to the 1975 FA Cup final, how many
games did Fulham play, excluding the final
itself?
    A. 7
    B. 9
    C. 11

40. When did Mohamed Al Fayed take control of
the club?
    A. 1995
    B. 1997
    C. 1999

Here are your answers to the last ten questions.

A31. At the end of the 2008/09 season, Fulham finished the campaign 7th in the Premier League; their highest ever finish, and they subsequently qualified for European competition the following season.

A32. Roy Hodgson was the manager for the 2008/09 campaign when Fulham finished 7th; their highest ever finishing position.

A33. In finishing 7th, Fulham amassed 53 points, their highest number of points in the top flight.

A34. Fulham won the Intertoto Cup in 2002.

A35. Fulham defeated Bologna in the two legged final.

A36. The first leg in Bologna was a 2-2 draw, and Fulham won the second leg at home, well at Loftus Road which was considered home for the season, 3-1 for an aggregate score of 5-3.

A37. Fulham have reached the semi finals of the FA Cup six times - in 1908, 1936, 1958, 1962, 1975 and 2002.

A38. Fulham have appeared in one very memorable FA Cup final - back in 1975.

A39. In typical Fulham-ish fashion, the club played a record 11 times en route to Wembley Stadium, due to the number of replays. Two replays were needed against Hull City in the third round; three replays against Nottingham Forest in the fourth round, and one replay against Birmingham City in the semi-final. As an aside, Bobby Moore started in each of these 11 games, and of course the Final.

A40. Mohamed Al Fayed took control of the club in the summer of 1997.

I hope you're having fun, and getting most of the answers right.

41. On his arrival, what did Al Fayed promise?
      A. All out attacking football
      B. Kids aged under 10 get free entry
      C. Top flight football within five years

42. What is the record transfer fee paid by the club?
      A. £21.7 million
      B. £22.8 million
      C. £23.9 million

43. Who was the record transfer fee paid for?
      A. Konstantinos Mitroglou
      B. Jean Michael Seri
      C. Andre-Frank Zambo Anguissa

44. What is the record transfer fee received by the club?
      A. £21 million
      B. £23 million
      C. £25 million

45. Who was the record transfer fee received for?
      A. Mousa Dembele
      B. Louis Saha
      C. Ryan Sessegnon

46. Who won the most international caps whilst a Fulham player?
      A. Johnny Haynes

B. Bobby Moore
C. Edwin van der Sar

47. Who was the club's first ever £1 million pound signing?
    A. Chris Coleman
    B. Barry Hayles
    C. Paul Peschisolido

48. Who is the youngest player ever to represent the club?
    A. Danny Briggs
    B. James Briggs
    C. Matthew Briggs

49. Who was the captain for the 1975 FA Cup Final?
    A. John Lacy
    B. Booby Moore
    C. Alan Mullery

50. Who was the manager at the 1975 FA Cup Final?
    A. Vic Buckingham
    B. Bobby Campbell
    C. Alec Stock

Here is the latest set of answers.

A41. He promised top flight football in five years!

A42. On the last day of the August 2018 transfer window Fulham paid £22.8 million for a defensive midfielder.

A43. The fee was paid to Marseille for Cameron international midfielder Andre-Frank Zambo Anguissa.

A44. The record transfer fee received by Fulham is £25 million.

A45. A reported £25 million was received from Tottenham Hotspur on 8th August 2019 for Ryan Sessegnon. This eclipsed the previous record of £18 million that was received from Tottenham Hotspur in August 2012 for Mousa Dembele.

A46. Haynes won 56 caps for England while he was at Fulham. Legend.

A47. Paul Peschisolido cost £1.1 million when he signed from West Bromwich Albion. He was the club's first £1 million plus signing.

A48. Matthew Briggs is the youngest player ever to represent the club. On making his first team debut at the age of 16 years, 65 days against Middlesbrough on 13th May 2007, he became both the club's and the Premier League's youngest ever player. He played 13 times for Fulham, and has since played for Leyton Orient, Peterborough United, Bristol City, Watford, Millwall and Colchester United. Not bad for a lad born in 1991.

A49. Alan Mullery wore the captain's arm band for the 1975 FA Cup Final.

A50. West Countryman Alec Stock got Fulham to Wembley for the 1975 FA Cup Final.

I hope you're learning some new facts about the club. Onto the next set of questions.

51. What are the club's cheerleaders known as?
    A. The SW6ers
    B. The Cottagers
    C. The Cravenettes

52. Who is the club's longest serving manager of all time?
    A. Phil Kelso
    B. Frank Osborne
    C. Jack Peart

53. Who is the oldest player ever to represent the club?
    A. Harold Crockford
    B. Mark Schwarzer
    C. Jimmy Sharp

54. What is the name of the Fulham home programme?
    A. Fulham Diaries
    B. Full Time
    C. The Official Fulham FC Matchday Programme

55. What is the nearest tube station to the ground?
    A. Fulham Broadway
    B. Parsons Green
    C. Putney Bridge

56. Which of these is a Fulham fanzine?

A. View from the cottage
B. When skies are grey
C. There's only one F in Fulham

57. What is on the club badge?
    A. A cottage
    B. FFC
    C. Two crossed swords

58. What is the club's motto?
    A. Consectatio Excellentiae
    B. Pro Civibus et Civitate
    C. There isn't a motto

59. Who is considered as Fulham's main rivals?
    A. Brentford
    B. Chelsea
    C. Queens Park Rangers

60. What could be regarded as the club's most well known chant?
    A. Can't Take My Eyes Off You
    B. The Sun Ain't Gonna Shine Anymore
    C. Silence is Golden

Here are the answers to the last set of questions.

A51. For reasons best known to themselves, The Cravenettes changed their name to the SW6ers.

A52. Phil Kelso is the club's longest serving manager of all time. He served from 1909 to 1924.

A53. In April 1920, Jimmy Sharp had just turned 40 years old when he played for the club - the oldest outfield player to play for the club. His record as oldest player ever to represent the club was taken by Mark Schwarzer who appeared for the club at the age of 40 years and 194 days against Swansea City on 19th May 2013.

A54. The catchy name of the Fulham match day programme is 'The official Fulham FC matchday programme'.

A55. Putney Bridge is the nearest tube station to Fulham's ground, whereas Fulham Broadway is the nearest tube station to Chelsea's ground.

A56. There's only one F in Fulham is the best known of the Fulham fanzines. It was established in 1988, and these days it has its own website too.

A57. Since 2001, Fulham's badge has consisted of a stylised shield with an angled red FFC on a black and white striped background.

A58. Fulham FC does not have a motto. Pro Civibus et Civitate, translated as "for citizens and state" is the motto of the London Borough of Hammersmith and Fulham.

A59. Chelsea is of course Fulham's main rival.

A60. All three songs listed were written by Bob Crewe and of course it's "Can't take my eyes off you" that can be regarded as the club's most well known chant. All together now "I thank God I'm alive...."

Let's give you some easier questions.

61. What is the traditional colour of the home shirt?
    A. Blue
    B. Red
    C. White

62. Who is the current club sponsor?
    A. BetVictor
    B. Dafabet
    C. Visit Florida

63. Who was the first club shirt sponsor?
    A. William Shatner
    B. William Shakespeare
    C. William Younger

64. Which pizza company once sponsored the club?
    A. Domino's Pizza
    B. Pizza Express
    C. Pizza Hut

65. Which of these sports brands has not supplied kit to Fulham?
    A. Admiral
    B. Le Coq Sportif
    C. Umbro

66. Who is currently the club chairman?
    A. Chaka Khan
    B. Genghis Khan

C. Shahid Khan

67. Who was the club's first foreign signing?
   A. Hassan Hegazi
   B. Ibrahim Hassan
   C. Tewfik Abdallah

68. When did Fulham start wearing white and black for the first time?
   A. 1900
   B. 1903
   C. 1906

69. Who was the club's first ever match in the league against?
   A. Accrington Stanley
   B. Bradford Park Avenue
   C. Hull City

70. What position did Fulham finish at the end of the 2019/20 season?
   A. 4th
   B. 5th
   C. 6th

Here are the answers to the last set of questions.

A61. The traditional colour of the home shirt is of course white.

A62. BetVictor is the current official club sponsor.

A63. Scottish brewers William Younger was the first shirt sponsor of Fulham - back in 1984.

A64. Pizza Hut sponsored the club from 2001 to 2002. Their corporate colours are red, white and black.

A65. Admiral has never supplied kit to Fulham whereas Le Coq Sportif and Umbro have. Other kit suppliers include Adidas, Airness, Kappa, Nike, Osca, Scoreline, Puma and Ribero.

A66. Pakistan born Shahid Khan is the current owner and chairman, having bought the club outright in July 2013.

A67. Egyptian Hassan Hegazi was the club's first foreign signing. He made just one solitary appearance for the club back in 1911 so if you get this question right, you can give yourself a bonus point.

A68. Initially Fulham played in combinations of red and white, or red, white and black while even navy blue made an appearance during the 1898/99 season. It wasn't until the 1903/04 campaign that Fulham first wore white shirts and black shorts.

A69. The club's first ever match in the League was against Hull City which was played on 3rd September 1907 with Fulham losing the match 1-0. Fulham's first ever win came a few days later, when they beat Derby County 1-0 on the 7th September 1907.

A70. Fulham finished the 2019/2020 season in 4th position in the Championship, and were promoted to the Premier League through the play-offs.

Here is the next batch of ten carefully chosen questions.

71. What is the biggest gap, in points, that Fulham have ever finished ahead of Chelsea?
    A. 14
    B. 18
    C. 22

72. Which of these brands is the current kit manufacturer?
    A. Adidas
    B. Nike
    C. Puma

73. Which famous Jimmy used to play for Fulham?
    A. Jimmy Choo
    B. Jimmy Connors
    C. Jimmy Hill

74. Which famous Rodney used to play for Fulham?
    A. Rodney Bewes
    B. Rodney Marsh
    C. Rodney Trotter

75. During the 2002/03 and 2003/04 seasons, with which London club did Fulham ground share?
    A. Brentford
    B. Crystal Palace
    C. Queens Park Rangers

76. Who was the first manager of the club?
    A. Harry Bradshaw
    B. Andy Decat
    C. Phil Kelso

77. Who started the 2020/21 season as manager?
    A. Stuart Gray
    B. Scott Parker
    C. Claudio Ranieri

78. What shirt number does defender Tim Ream wear?
    A. 13
    B. 14
    C. 15

79. Which of these played in goal for Fulham?
    A. David de Gea
    B. Ed de Goey
    C. Edwin van der Sar

80. Which of these actors is a Fulham fan?
    A. Keith Allen
    B. Hugh Grant
    C. Daniel Radcliffe

Here are the answers to the last ten questions.

A71. At the end of the 1981/82 campaign, Fulham finished 14 places and 22 points ahead of Chelsea, in the old Division Two - what is now the Championship.

A72. Adidas is the current kit manufacturer.

A73. It is of course ex-chairman Jimmy Hill who used to play for the club. In his playing days, he made 276 appearances for the club and once scored five goals in one game.

A74. Rodney Marsh played a total of 79 games in his two spells with Fulham. The maverick striker won 9 England caps in his career.

A75. Fulham shared QPR's ground at Loftus Road for two seasons, whilst improvements were made at Craven Cottage to upgrade the ground and turn it into an all seater stadium.

A76. Harry Bradshaw was the first full time manager of the club. He managed the club from 1904 to 1909.

A77. Scott Parker started the 2020/21 campaign as manager, having been appointed to the job in February 2019.

A78. Defender Tim Ream wears the number 13 shirt.

A79. Edwin van der Sar joined Fulham on 1st August 2001 from Juventus for a fee in the region of £7 million. He notched up 127 league appearances before he was sold to Manchester United.

A80. They are all Fulham supporters! Give yourself a bonus point if you thought that.

Here are the next set of questions, let's hope you get most of them right.

81. What was the club's lowest ever finish - in the bottom division, back in May 1996?
    A. 15th
    B. 16th
    C. 17th

82. In the Great Escape of 2008 who did Fulham beat 1-0 in the last game of the 2007/08 season to stay up?
    A. Birmingham City
    B. Portsmouth
    C. Reading

83. Which of these ex-players went on to manage England?
    A. Chris Coleman
    B. Bobby Robson
    C. Graham Taylor

84. What is the lowest ever attendance for a first class game at Craven Cottage?
    A. 2,176
    B. 4,182
    C. 8,472

85. When did Fulham reach the top tier of English football for the first time?
    A. 1921
    B. 1935

C. 1949

86. Who is the highest goal scorer for the club in the *Premier League era*?
   A. Clint Dempsey
   B. Brian McBride
   C. Louis Saha

87. Who was the manager as Fulham won League Two in 1998/99?
   A. Chris Coleman
   B. Kevin Keegan
   C. Malcolm McDonald

88. Who was known as "The Maestro"?
   A. Jimmy Bullard
   B. Johnny Byrne
   C. Johnny Haynes

89. Who was known as the 'The Galloping Hairpin'?
   A. Jim Hammond
   B. Bedford Jezzard
   C. Jim Langley

90. Who scored 12 goals in the 1981/82 season - a club record for a defender?
   A. Roger Brown
   B. Tony Gale
   C. Robert Wilson

Here are the answers to the last block of questions.

A81. At the end of the 1995/96 season Fulham finished 17th out of the 24 teams in Football League Division Three- akin to the old Fourth Division, being the fourth tier. So that's 85th out of all 92 clubs in the four leagues. During the season, in January, they were second from bottom - the club's lowest ever league position.

A82. In the Great Escape of 2008, Danny Murphy's late goal at Fratton Park, Portsmouth - the only goal of the game, enabled Fulham to retain their Premier League status by the skin of their teeth - on goal difference.

A83. Sir Bobby Robson, who served Fulham with such distinction as both a player and a manager, later went on to manage England.

A84. Only 2,176 turned up to see Fulham lose at home to Scunthorpe on the 30th January 1996. Dark days indeed.

A85. Fulham ended the 19948/49 season as Division Two champions, and thus earning promotion to the top tier of English football for the first time. They took their bow in August 1949 and finished the season 17th, out of the 22 sides in Division One.

A86. With 50 Premier League goals, Clint Dempsey is the highest goal scorer for the club in the Premier

League era. Joint second with 32 goals are Steed Malbranque and Brian McBride, with Louis Saha and Luis Boa Morte scoring 26 each.

A87. With Kevin Keegan as manager, Fulham romped to the 1998/99 League Two title with an astonishing 101 points.

A88. It was of course Johnny Haynes who was known as the "Maestro". Pele was once quoted as calling Haynes the "best passer of the ball I've ever seen."

A89. Jim Hammond was nicknamed 'The galloping hairpin' because of his unusual physique. He was a born goal scorer with a fierce shot, playing 342 games and scoring 150 goals for the club between 1928 and 1938.

A90. Roger Brown scored 12 goals in the successful promotion winning campaign of 1981/82 - a record for a Fulham defender in a single campaign, which is still intact today.

Here is the final set of questions. Enjoy!

91. How many games did Fulham play in the 2009/10 Europa League?
    A. 11
    B. 15
    C. 19

92. During the 2009/10 Europa League run, which Italian club did Fulham knock out of the competition?
    A. Inter Milan
    B. Juventus
    C. Napoli

93. Where was the 2010 Europa League Final played?
    A. Berlin
    B. Hamburg
    C. Munich

94. Who was captain for the 2010 Europa League Final?
    A. Chris Baird
    B. Brede Hangeland
    C. Danny Murphy

95. Who scored in the 2010 Europa League final?
    A. Damien Duff
    B. Simon Davies
    C. Bobby Zamora

96. Who scored the winning goal in the 2019/20
Championship play-off Final?
   A. Joe Bryan
   B. Aleksandar Mitrovic
   C. Josh Onomah

97. In 1926 Fulham became the first British club to
do what?
   A. Let ladies in for free
   B. Sell hot dogs outside the ground
   C. Install floodlighting

98. Which musician once had a statue outside the
ground?
   A. Louis Armstrong
   B. Michael Jackson
   C. Barry White

99. Which player started the 2020/21 season as
captain?
   A. Tom Cairney
   B. Maxime Le Marchand
   C. Tim Ream

100. Who is the only player who has played for the
club in all four leagues?
   A. Sean Davis
   B. Clint Dempsey
   C. Steed Malbranque

101. Which ex-player has a magnificent statue
outside the ground?
   A. George Best

B. Johnny Haynes
C. Bobby Moore

Here goes with the last set of answers.

A91. Fulham played an incredible 19 games in the 2009/10 Europa League campaign, including two qualifying round matches, two play off round matches and then six group games, before even qualifying for the knockout stages of the competition.

A92. Fulham knocked out 30 times Serie A winners Juventus in the round of 16. Having lost the first leg 3-1 in Turin, in one of the most memorable nights in Fulham's history, the Whites produced a stunning comeback to win the second leg 4-1, and the tie 5-4 on aggregate.

A93. The 2010 Europa League final was played at the HSH Nordbank Arena in Hamburg.

A94. The captain for the season including for the Europa League Final was Danny Murphy. He played over 150 matches for the club between 2007 and 2012.

A95. Midfielder Simon Davies scored the equalising goal in the 37th minute.

A96. In the Championship play- off Final on 4th August 2020, Joe Bryan scored both goals in a 2-1 victory over Brentford to secure promotion to the Premier League.

A97. Fulham were the first British club to sell hot dogs at their ground.

A98. A plaster and resin statue of Michael Jackson was controversially unveiled in April 2011. It was removed in September 2013, and now stands at the National Football Museum in Manchester if you want to see it.

A99. Tom Cairney started the 2020/21 season as captain.

A100. Sean Davis played in all four leagues for the club. He made a total of 155 appearances for the club between 1996 and 2004.

A101. In October 2008, the club unveiled a magnificent bronze statue of the one and only Johnny Haynes which stands proudly outside the Cottage Gates outside the ground. If only he was playing for Fulham now!

Johnny Haynes seems a fitting place to finish this quiz. I hope you enjoyed this ebook, and I hope you got most of the answers right. I also hope you learnt a few new things about the club.

If you see anything wrong, or have a general comment, please visit the glowwormpress.com website.

Thanks for reading, and to show your support for this great club, would you please leave a positive review for this book on Amazon.

Printed in Great Britain
by Amazon

49461647R00028